PASTA
& SEAFOOD

now you're cookin'

Colophon

© 2002 Rebo International b.v., Lisse, The Netherlands

This 2nd edition reprinted in 2006.

Original recipes and photos: © R&R Publishing Pty. Ltd.

Design and layout: Minkowsky Graphics, Enkhuizen, The Netherlands

Typesetting: AdAm Studio, Prague, The Czech Republic

Cover design: Minkowsky Graphics, Enkhuizen, The Netherlands

ISBN 13: 978-90-366-1617-1

ISBN 10: 90-366-1617-4

now you're cookin' PASTA & SEAFOOD

THIS BOOK JUST MAKES YOU WANNA COOK

REBO PUBLISHERS

Foreword

In the beginning, there was waving grain. Then came man who transformed the grain into pasta, in all shapes and sizes. Behind the mountains was the sea. In that sea there was a miraculous world of fauna. Man picked these fruits of the sea, enchanted by their beauty. One day, a little man had an idea - he was small but he knew what was good - he took the gold of the earth and the jewels of the sea. He carried them home and put everything in a big pan. It was that day that land and sea met and fused together. Such a delicious thing no-one had ever tasted. Since then, many variations have been created, the best of which you will find in this book. From Fettuccine with seafood and Salmon ravioli with lemon-dill sauce to Linguine with garlic oysters and Spaghetti with squid and coriander.

Abbreviations

All measurements conform to European
and American measurement systems.
For easier cooking, the American cup
measurement is used throughout the book.

tbsp = tablespoon

tsp = teaspoon

oz = ounce

lb = pound

°F = degrees Fahrenheit

°C = degrees Celsius

g = gram

kg = kilogram

cm = centimeter

ml = mililiter

l = liter

Method

Bring a large saucepan of water to boil. Using a strainer, carefully lower calamari into water. Cook for 5-10 seconds or until it just turns white and is firm. Drain. Plunge into iced water. Drain again. Set aside.

Bring a large saucepan of fresh water to boil. Add pasta. Cook according to packet directions.

Meanwhile, place oil, onion and garlic in a nonstick frying pan over a medium heat. Cook, stirring, for 3-4 minutes or until onion is soft. Add tomatoes, olives, stock and wine. Bring to simmering. Simmer for 5 minutes. Stir in coriander, mint, calamari and black pepper to taste. Cook for 1-2 minutes or until heated through.

Drain pasta. Add calamari mixture. Toss to combine.

To serve, divide pasta mixture between serving bowls.

Accompany with crusty Italian bread and a green salad.

Calamari and Coriander Spaghetti

Ingredients

16oz/500g calamari (squid), cleaned, tube cut into rings

16oz/500g spaghetti or vermicelli

2 tsp olive oil

1 red onion, finely diced

1 clove garlic, crushed

4 plum tomatoes, seeded and diced

½ cup/80g cored black olives, rinsed and drained, sliced

¼ cup/60ml low-salt chicken or fish stock (page 174)

¼ cup/60ml dry white wine

1 cup/50g chopped fresh coriander

3 tbsp chopped fresh mint

freshly ground black pepper

Method

Brown the sliced garlic in olive oil. Stir in the parsley and chopped anchovies. Add water to cover, and simmer for a few minutes. Meanwhile, cook the pasta in boiling salted water until al dente.

Drain the pasta.

Ingredients

1lb/500g linguini pasta

4 cloves garlic, minced

6 tbsp olive oil

2 tbsp fresh parsley, chopped

3x 2oz/55g cans anchovy filets, chopped

1 cup water

Anchovy Linguini

Method

Preheat the oven to 400 °F/200 °C. Cook the pasta in plenty of boiling salted water, until tender but still firm to the bite. Drain and return to the saucepan. Set aside 1 tablespoon each of the Gruyère, Cheddar and dill, then mix the rest into the pasta with the crème fraîche and cayenne.

Grease a 8 x 6in/20 x 15cm ovenproof dish with half the butter, then spoon in half the pasta. Lay the salmon strips on top and cover with the remaining pasta. Sprinkle with the reserved Gruyère, Cheddar and dill, then dot with the remaining butter. Cover with foil, then bake for 15 minutes. Remove the foil and bake for additional minutes or until the top is bubbling and golden.

Baked Rigatoni with Smoked Salmon

Ingredients

14oz/400g dried pasta
tubes (rigatoni)

salt

5oz/150g Gruyère,
coarsely grated

5oz/150g reduced-fat Cheddar,
coarsely grated

2 tbsp chopped fresh dill

7fl oz/200ml carton crème fraîche

1 tsp cayenne pepper

1oz/25g butter

9oz/250g smoked salmon,
cut into strips

Mehod

Cook the fettucine in boiling water until al dente, drain.

Meanwhile, heat the oil in a large frying pan over moderate heat.

Add the garlic, cook for 2 minutes.

Add the cooked fettucine, chives, red and black caviar and eggs,

toss well and heat through. Top with sour cream and serve.

Fettucine with Caviar

Ingredients

11oz/315g fettucine

4 tbsp olive oil

2 cloves garlic, crushed

2 tbsp snipped fresh chives

3 tbsp red caviar

3 tbsp black caviar

2 hard-boiled eggs, chopped

2fl oz/60ml sour cream

Method

Add 1 tablespoon of the olive oil to a large pot of lightly salted water, and bring to a boil. Add the pasta, and cook until al dente and drain. To keep the pasta from sticking together, rinse it quickly with cold water.

Heat the remaining olive oil in a 10in/25cm skillet. Cook the garlic over medium heat, stirring constantly until the garlic is tender, about 1 minute. Do not let the garlic burn. Add the shrimps, and continue stirring until pink, about 3-5 minutes. Remove the shrimp from the skillet, and set aside.

Stir the tomatoes, wine, parsley and basil into the skillet. Continue cooking, stirring occasionally, until liquid is reduced by half, 8-12 minutes. Return the shrimps to the skillet, and continue cooking until the prawns are heated through, about 2-3 minutes. Serve the shrimp mixture over the pasta. Top with Parmesan cheese.

Ingredients

¼ cup light olive oil

8oz/225g package angel hair pasta

1 tsp garlic, chopped

1lb/500g large shrimps, peeled and deveined

2x 26oz/750g cans Italian-style diced tomatoes,

drained

½ cup dry white wine

¼ cup chopped parsley

3 tbsp chopped fresh basil

3 tbsp grated Parmesan cheese

Angel Hair Pasta with Shrimp and Basil

Method

Bring a large pot of lightly salted water to a boil. Add the pasta and cook for 8-10 minutes or until al dente; drain.

In a small saucepan, boil the squid in 3 cups of water mixed with the red wine vinegar for 8-10 minutes. Drain, cut into bite-sized rings pieces, and set aside.

Heat the olive oil in a large heavy skillet. Sauté the onion and garlic until onion is tender, but not brown. Stir in the squid, and sauté for 2 minutes. Pour in the crushed tomatoes, white wine and lemon juice. Season with cinnamon stick, bay leaves, basil, oregano, salt and pepper. Bring to a boil, reduce heat, and simmer 15-20 minutes partially covered, stirring occasionally.

Remove from heat, and mix in cooked pasta.

Serve topped with grated cheese.

Calamari Macaronatha

Ingredients

2½ cup elbow macaroni	¼ cup dry white wine
1lb/500g squid, cleaned	½ lemon, juiced
¼ cup red wine vinegar	1 cinnamon stick, broken in half
6 tbsp extra virgin olive oil	2 bay leaves
4 cloves garlic, minced	¼ tsp dried basil leaves
1 large onion, chopped	½ tsp dried oregano
1½ cup crushed tomatoes	salt and ground black pepper to taste
	½ cup grated Myzithra cheese

Method

Cook the pasta in boiling water in a large saucepan following the packet directions. Drain, rinse under cold running water, then drain, again and set aside to cool completely.

Place the avocado, orange zest, orange juice and black pepper to taste in a food processor or blender and process until smooth.

Place the pasta in a bowl, top with avocado mixture, and toss to combine. Roll salmon slices into cornets and fill with a dill sprig. Divide the salad between four serving plates and top with the salmon cornets and orange segments.

Ingredients

13oz/370g bow pasta

1 large avocado, stoned, peeled and roughly chopped

1 tsp finely grated orange zest

2 tbsp fresh orange juice

freshly ground black pepper

4 slices smoked salmon

4 sprigs fresh dill

1 orange, segmented

Avocado Salmon Salad

Method

Preheat the oven to 350°F/180°C. Cook the cannelloni in boiling
salted water until al dente. Drain and cool.

Sauté the cannelloni in hot oil for 5 minutes until crisp. Remove and drain
on paper towels.

Combine the crabmeat, mayonnaise, pepper to taste and lemon juice and spoon
into cannelloni tubes. Place the filled cannelloni tubes in a shallow ovenproof dish,
sprinkle with paprika and bake for 15 minutes or until heated through.
Serve with curly endive and cherry tomatoes.

Cannelloni with Crab and Curly Endive

Ingredients

12 large cannelloni tubes

oil for frying

12/3lb/750g crabmeat

8oz/225g mayonnaise

freshly ground black pepper

2 tbsp freshly squeezed lemon juice

paprika

curly endive

8oz/225g cherry tomatoes

21

Method

In a small saucepan, melt 2 tablespoons butter or margarine.

Stir in flour to make a paste. Set roux aside.

Sauté the mushrooms, Cajun spice, and garlic in ¼ cup butter

or margarine over medium-high heat for 2 minutes. Add the oysters,

corn, string beans, and pimiento. Sauté for 1½ minutes. Add the stock

and linguine, and bring to a slight simmer.

Fold in roux until the sauce thickens, then reduce heat. Fold in the

parsley and spring onions. Fold in a lump of the crabmeat, and heat

through. Serve immediately.

Ingredients

¼ cup butter

8oz/225g fresh mushrooms, quartered

1 tsp Cajun seasoning

1 tsp minced garlic

24 shucked oysters, quartered

½ cup whole corn kernels, blanched

2/3 cup French cut green beans

Garlic Oyster Linguini

2 tbsp chopped pimiento peppers

½ cup seafood stock

10oz/285g fresh linguine pasta

2 tbsp butter

2 tbsp plain flour

2 tbsp chopped fresh parsley

3 tbsp thinly sliced spring onion

4oz/115g crabmeat

Method

Place the sultanas in a bowl, cover with hot water and leave to soak for 15 minutes or until they plump up. Drain well. Heat a large heavy-based frying pan over a high heat, then add the pine nut kernels and dry-fry for 2-3 minutes, until golden. Remove from the pan and set aside. Cook the broccoli florets in boiling salted water for 3 minutes, then drain well.

Heat the oil in the frying pan, then gently fry the onion for 5 minutes or until softened. Add the anchovies and mash well with a fork, then stir in the broccoli, sultanas and pine nut kernels and cook, stirring, for 5 minutes. Season to taste.

Cook the pasta in plenty of boiling salted water, until tender but still firm to the bite. Drain, return to the pan, then toss with the butter, Parmesan and half the broccoli mixture. Transfer to a bowl and top with the remaining broccoli mixture.

Conchiglie with Broccoli and Sultanas

Ingredients

3 tbsp sultanas

2 tbsp pine nut kernels

1lb 2oz/500g broccoli, cut into florets, thick stem discarded

salt and black pepper

4 tbsp extra virgin olive oil

1 small onion, thinly sliced

4 anchovy fillets, drained and chopped

14oz/400g dried pasta shells (conchiglie)

1oz/25g butter

2oz/50g Parmesan, freshly grated

Method

Heat the oil in a large skillet over medium high heat. Add the garlic and sauté for 30 seconds. Add the shrimp and sauté until almost cooked through, about 2 minutes. Add the artichokes, feta, tomatoes, lemon juice, parsley and oregano and sauté until the shrimps are cooked through, about 2 minutes. Season with salt and pepper.

Meanwhile, cook the pasta in large pot of boiling salted water until just tender but still firm to bite, stirring occasionally. Drain. Transfer the pasta to large bowl.

Add the shrimp mixture to the pasta and toss to coat. Season to taste with salt and pepper and serve.

Ingredients

¼ cup olive oil

4 tsp garlic, minced

1 lb/500g uncooked medium shrimps, peeled, deveined

1½ cup drained canned artichoke hearts, chopped

1½ cup crumbled feta cheese

½ cup chopped seeded tomatoes

3 tbsp fresh lemon juice

3 tbsp chopped fresh parsley

2 tbsp finely chopped fresh oregano or 1½ tsp dried

Greek-Style Pasta with Shrimps

Method

Finely chop the shrimp. Place the shrimp, garlic, ginger and spring onions

in a bowl and mix to combine.

Put a teaspoon of the mixture in the center of a wonton wrapper, lightly brush

the edges with water and top with another wrapper. Press the edges firmly

together to seal. Repeat with the remaining filling and wrappers.

Cook the ravioli in batches in a large pot of rapidly boiling water for 5 minutes.

Drain well and transfer to serving plates.

To make the dressing – put the chilli, fish sauce, palm sugar, lime juice

and peanut oil in a jar and whisk to combine.

Drizzle the dressing over the ravioli and serve topped with sprigs

of fresh coriander.

Shrimp and Ginger Ravioli

Ingredinets

4½ cup/600g green shrimps,

peeled and deveined

1 clove garlic, chopped

1 tbsp grated fresh ginger

2 spring onions, finely sliced

7oz/200g wonton wrappers

fresh coriander sprigs, to garnish

Dressing

1 small red chili, finely sliced

2 tbsp fish sauce

2 tsp grated palm sugar

2 tsp lime juice

1 tbsp peanut oil

Method

Heat olive oil on medium-high heat in a large frypan or wok. Add the shallots and garlic. Sauté for 1 minute or until softened slightly, then add lemon rind, parsley, shrimp and scallops. Sauté together until the shrimps just turn pink and scallops are translucent, about 1-2 minutes. Remove with a drainer from pan. Season with salt and pepper.

Add the white wine to pan, bring to boil and add mussels. Cover and steam the mussels until they open, about 3 minutes. Remove the mussels from pan and reserve with *shrimp* and scallops. Discard any mussels that do not open. Remove mussel meats from half the mussels, leaving the rest in their shells. Meanwhile drain the tomatoes and chop, reserving juice. Add the tomatoes, juice and chili flakes into pan and bring to boil. Stir in half the basil and simmer for 10 minutes to combine flavors. Season with salt and pepper. The sauce can be made ahead to this point.

When ready to serve, bring a large pot of salted water to boil.

Add the pasta and cook until al dente, about 10-12 minutes. Drain well.

Return the seafood to sauce, sprinkle with remaining basil then reheat.

Toss with the pasta and serve.

Ingredients

2 tbsp olive oil	12 scallops
3 shallots chopped, or spring onions	½ cup white wine
1 tsp grated lemon rind	2lb mussels
½ tsp red chili pepper flakes	26oz/750g tomatoes, canned
2 tbsp parsley, chopped	¼ cup basil, fresh, shredded
12 large shrimp	1lb linguini

Linguini with Seafood

Note

Vary the seafood according to your taste. If you
prefer a vegetarian version, sauté the mushrooms
and capsicum (Bell peppers) instead of seafood and
add into the tomato sauce. Grated Parmesan
is traditionally not offered with seafood dishes.
Also it's a great idea to serve the pasta and sauce
in a large bowl on the table and let people
help themselves.

pasta & seafood

Method

Bring a large saucepan of lightly salted water to a boil, add penne,

cook until al dente.

Meanwhile, melt the butter in a heavy-based saucepan over moderate heat.

Add the spring onions, cook 2 minutes. Add the orange zest, fennel seeds

and mussels. Cover, cook 5 minutes, remove opened mussels. Cook additional

3 minutes, remove remaining opened mussels. Discard any mussels that have

not opened.

Remove the mussels from their shells and set aside. Reserve a few shells

for garnish if desired.

Add the cream to the pan, boil until sauce thickens. Season to taste with

pepper. Reduce heat, return the mussels to the sauce, heat through very gently.

Drain the penne thoroughly, place in a large, heated bowl. Remove the orange

strips from the sauce, pour the sauce over penne. Toss well to mix.

Serve immediately.

Penne with Mussels in Orange Cream Sauce

Ingredients

1lb/500g penne

3oz/85g unsalted butter

8 spring onions, chopped

6 strips orange zest

¼ tsp fennel seeds

4½lb/2kg mussels, scrubbed and debearded

8fl oz/225ml heavy cream

freshly ground black pepper

Method

Over a medium heat, in a medium size sauce pan, melt the whole butter and add the lobster stock and the cream and turn heat up to medium high.

When cream is hot, just before boiling, add the Parmesan cheese and whisk briskly until all the cheese is melted and dissolved into the cream. Add the Worcestershire, Tabasco, black pepper and Dijon and whisk thoroughly again. Reduce heat again to a fast simmer and allow mixture to simmer 20 minutes.

Cook pasta to your taste, while the sauce is simmering, drain and set onto plates. Cut the lobster meat into small pieces and add to sauce, add the egg yolks and turn heat to medium high. Sauce should be of medium thickness. Ladle sauce over the pasta, sprinkle with fresh chopped parsley and serve.

Ingredients

½ cup lobster stock, or fish stock

1 tsp Dijon mustard

1 cup fresh shucked lobster meat

¼ tsp Tabasco

1¼ cup freshly grated Parmesan cheese

¼ tsp black pepper

Lobster Alfredo

pasta & seafood

1 tbsp whole butter

2 cup heavy cream

4 each egg yolks

¼ cup fresh chopped parsley

1 dash Worcestershire sauce

¾ lb/340g fettucine pasta

Method

Prepare the pasta according to package directions. While the pasta is cooking, heat 1 tablespoon of oil in a large frypan or wok. Add the red onion and cook for about 2 minutes. Add the scallops, corn and garlic. Cook for 4 minutes, stirring often. Add the tomatoes, oregano, rosemary and hot sauce. Simmer just until the scallops are done and mixture is thoroughly heated, about 5 minutes. Stir in 2 tablespoons of the red wine vinegar and lemon juice.

Drain well when the pasta is done. Transfer to a serving bowl. Drizzle with the remaining 1 teaspoon oil and toss well. Spoon the tomato mixture over pasta.

Sprinkle with cheese, salt and pepper and serve immediately.

Fresh Corn, Tomato & Scallop Pasta

Ingredients

1lb/500g medium shells, ziti or other medium pasta shape, uncooked

1 tbs plus 1 tsp olive or vegetable oil

¾ cup sliced red onion

1lb/500g scallops or medium shrimp , peeled and deveined

1 cup fresh or frozen corn kernels (2 ears)

2 cloves garlic, minced

4 large ripe tomatoes, peeled, seeded and diced (4 cups)

2 tbsp minced fresh oregano

½ tsp dried rosemary

½-1 tsp Tabasco sauce

2 tbsp red wine vinegar

1 tbsp lemon juice

2oz/55g crumbled feta cheese

salt and freshly ground pepper to taste

Method

Combine 5 cups of the tangerine or orange juice, the yellow onion, jalapeño, bay leaves and 1 tablespoon of garlic in a medium saucepan. Bring to a boil and cook until liquid is reduced by two-thirds. Remove the bay leaves. Allow to cool. Transfer the juice mixture to a blender and blend until smooth. Add salt and pepper to taste and set aside.

Prepare the pasta according to package directions. While the pasta is cooking, add the oil, red onion and shrimp to a medium frypan. Sauté 1 minute. Add the remaining ½ cup tangerine or orange juice to the pan and cook over low heat.

Drain the pasta, return it to the pot and add the reserved orange sauce and the shrimp mixture. Cook over low heat 1 minute. Stir in the Brie and basil. Stir until the Brie is melted. Transfer to a serving bowl. Garnish with orange segments and toasted almonds. Serve immediately.

Ingredients

1lb/500g mostaccioli, ziti or other medium

pasta shape, uncooked

5½ cup tangerine or orange juice, divided

1 large yellow onion, minced

1 tbsp minced, seeded jalapeño pepper

2 bay leaves

2 tbsp minced garlic, divided

1 tbsp olive or vegetable oil

Mostaccioli and Shrimp with Tangerine Basil Sauce

1 medium red onion, thinly sliced

1lb medium shrimp , peeled and deveined

salt and freshly ground

pepper to taste

4oz/115g diced Brie cheese

2 tbsp thinly sliced basil leaves

1 cup tangerine or orange segments

⅓ cup slivered almonds, lightly toasted

pasta & seafood

Method

Preheat the oven to 350°F/180°C Prepare the pasta according
to package directions; drain.

Place the salmon in a non-reactive baking dish; season with pepper.
Cover with aluminum foil and bake for 25 minutes. Remove the foil
and cool. Remove the skin, bones and discard. Flake the salmon into
large pieces and place in a large mixing bowl (If using canned salmon,
place directly in the bowl and season with pepper). Add the dill, celery,
onion, carrot and pasta. In a small bowl, whisk together the oil, lemon
juice and vinegar. Add the salmon and pasta and toss gently.

Serve well chilled.

Ingredients

1lb/500g radiatore, wagon wheels

or other medium pasta shape, uncooked

1lb/500g salmon steaks,

or 14oz/400g can salmon,

drained freshly ground pepper

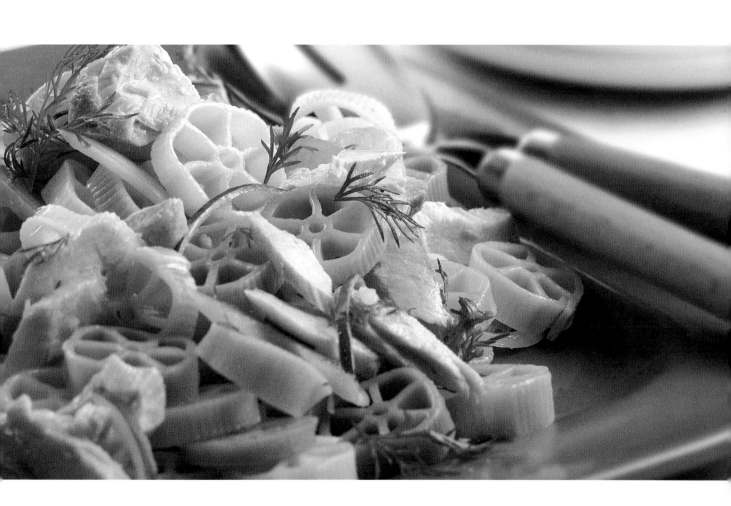

Pasta with Salmon and Dill

4 tbsp chopped fresh dill

3 stalks celery, chopped, about 1 cup

1 medium onion, chopped, about 1 cup

1 carrot, sliced

2 tbsp vegetable oil

2 tbsp lemon juice

1 tbsp white wine vinegar

Method

Cook the pasta according to the package directions and drain. Heat the oil in a large frypan or wok and add the celery, capsicum (Bell pepper), carrots and green onions.

Cook, tossing until crisp but tender. Slice the scallops in thirds (bay scallops can be used whole). Add to the vegetables and toss until opaque, about 1-2 minutes.

Add the orange juice, chili flakes and orange zest. Cook 2 more minutes; pour over the cooked pasta. Toss with cheese. Garnish with parsley.

Fettuccine with Vegetables and Scallops

Inngredients

12oz/340g fettuccine, uncooked	18oz/510g raw ocean scallops or bay scallops
2 tbsp olive or vegetable oil	½ cup fresh orange juice
2 stalks celery	red chili flakes to taste
1 red capsicum (Bell peppers)	1 tsp grated orange zest
2 carrots	¾ cup grated Romano cheese
3 spring onions	parsley for garnish

Method

Heat the butter in a pan and sauté the shallots and garlic until the garlic is golden. Add the fish pieces and sauté until almost cooked. Remove the fish and set aside. Keep warm.

With the heat on high add the wine to the pan and cook for approximately 2-3 minutes. Add the lemon juice, lemon slices, parsley, green peppercorns and salt to taste. Cook for approximately 5 minutes to reduce sauce to half its original quantity. Turn the heat to low and add the cream, simmer for additional 5 minutes. Remove the fish to the sauce and allow to heat through.

Serve immediately over the hot pasta, cooked al dente, and garnish with extra parsley.

Ingredients

1lb/500g penne pasta

2oz/55g butter

4 medium shallots, finely chopped

3 cloves garlic, crushed

1lb/500g firm, white fleshed fish (sea perch,

rockling, gem fish), cut into chunks

½ cup dry white wine

Penne with Fish and Lemon

2½ oz/75ml lemon juice

3 thin slices of lemon, with peel
removed from 2 slices

1 tbsp Italian parsley, finely chopped

½ tsp green peppercorns

salt to taste

11fl oz/310ml cream

extra parsley, chopped

Method

Bring a large pot of lightly salted water to a boil. Drop in the shrimp and scallops and simmer for 10 minutes; remove the seafood and reserve the seafood water or broth in another bowl.

In the same saucepan, melt the butter and add onion, garlic, red and green capsicum (pepper); sauté and stir until transparent, but do not brown.

Add the flour and mix well until all the vegetables are coated, add some seafood broth slowly, but stirring constantly. Add the imitation crabmeat and mix; add the milk, and salt, and pepper to taste and mix.

Add the marjoram, basil and tarragon and simmer very gently, stir constantly until the wanted thickness is obtained. Take off of heat and reserve.

Bring a large pot of lightly salted water to a boil.

Add the fettuccini and cook for 6-8 minutes or until al dente; drain and cover with the seafood sauce. Serve.

Fettuccine de la Mer

Ingredients

9oz/255g medium shrimp, peeled and deveined

9oz/255g scallops

2 tbsp butter

1 onion, chopped

1 clove garlic, minced

1 green capsicum (pepper), chopped

1 red capsicum (pepper), chopped

2 tbsp plain flour

9oz/255g imitation crabmeat

2 cup milk

salt and pepper to taste

1 pinch dried marjoram

1 pinch dried basil leaves

1 pinch dried tarragon

10oz/285g dry fettuccini noodles

Method

To make the mayonnaise, place raspberries in a food processor or blender and process until smooth. Push the purée through a fine sieve and discard seeds. Add the mayonnaise, mustard and lemon juice to purée, mix to combine and set aside.

Cook the pasta in boiling water in a large saucepan following the packet directions. Drain, set aside and keep warm.

Heat the oil in a frying or grill pan over a medium heat. Brush the salmon with lemon juice and sprinkle with dill. Place the salmon in the pan and cook for 2-3 minutes each side or until flesh flakes when tested with a fork. Remove the salmon from the pan and cut into thick slices.

To serve, divide the pasta between six serving plates. Top with the salmon slices and drizzle with raspberry mayonnaise. Serve immediately.

Ingredients

1lb/500g pepper or plain fettuccine

1 tbsp vegetable oil

1lb/500g salmon fillet, bones and skin removed

2 tbsp lemon juice

Raspberry Salmon Pasta

2 tbsp chopped fresh dill

raspberry mayonnaise

7oz/200g raspberries

1 cup low oil mayonnaise

2 tsp wholegrain mustard

1 tbsp lemon juice

Method

Cook the potatoes in a large pot of water until soft. Drain, return to the pot and cook over a low heat until dry. Remove from the heat and mash until smooth.

Put the vermicelli in a large bowl, cover with boiling water and set aside for 10 minutes or until soft. Drain well and cut into short pieces using kitchen scissors.

Put the potatoes, vermicelli, salmon, egg whites, corn, spring onions, capsicum (pepper), breadcrumbs, dill and lemon juice in a bowl and combine well.

Divide the mixture into eight and shape each portion into a flat patty. Put on a baking tray lined with non stick baking paper and refrigerate for 30 minutes or until firm. Preheat the oven to 400°F/200°C.

Lightly spray a non stick fry pan with olive oil spray and heat over a medium heat until hot. Cook the patties in batches until golden brown on both sides, transfer to the oven and cook for 10-15 minutes more or until heated through.

Ingredients

3 potatoes (about 14oz/400g), peeled and chopped

4oz/100g dry rice vermicelli

15oz/420g canned, no added salt red salmon

2 egg whites, lightly beaten

4oz/130g can creamed corn

4 spring onions, sliced

1 red capsicum (pepper), finely chopped

2 cup fresh breadcrumbs

2 tbsps chopped fresh dill

1-2 tbsps lemon juice

Salmon and Creamed Corn Patties

olive oil cooking spray

creamed corn patties

1 tbsp of butter or margarine

1 tbsp of flour

½ cup warm whole or half-fat milk

half-fat cream

8oz/225ml fresh corn grains

salt, white pepper

Method

Cook the pasta according to the instructions on the packet, until tender but firm to the bite. Drain, rinse under cold running water to cool, then drain thoroughly. Place in a serving bowl.

To make the dressing, whisk together the passata, olive oil, vinegar, sugar, basil and black pepper in a bowl until thoroughly mixed. Pour the dressing over the pasta, then toss to mix well.

Add the sliced spring onions, yellow pepper, sugar snap peas, sweetcorn and tuna to the pasta and toss lightly. Garnish with the spring onion strips.

Flaked Tuna Pasta Salad in Tomato Dressing

Ingredients

8oz/225g dried wholewheat pasta twists or shapes

4 spring onions, sliced, plus thin strips to garnish

1 yellow pepper, deseeded and diced

4oz/125g sugar snap peas, chopped

7oz/200g can sweetcorn, drained

6oz/185g can tuna in water, drained and flaked

For the dressing

5 tbsp passata

1 tbsp extra virgin olive oil

2 tsp balsamic vinegar

pinch of povdered sugar

2 tbsp chopped fresh basil

black pepper

Method

To make the sauce, heat the oil in a large saucepan and cook the onion, red capsicum (pepper), garlic, chili, cumin and ground coriander for 3-4 minutes or until the onion is soft. Add the tomatoes, wine and tomato paste and cook over a medium heat for 30 minutes longer or until sauce reduces and thickens.

Add the calamari to the sauce and cook for 5 minutes or until just tender. Add the mussels and shrimp and cook for 4-5 minutes longer. Mix in 2 tablespoons fresh coriander. Season to taste with black pepper.

Cook the fettuccine in boiling water in a large saucepan following the packet directions. Drain, then spoon the sauce over the fettuccine and sprinkle with the remaining fresh coriander. Serve immediately.

Ingredients

1lb/500g mixed colored fettuccine

spicy seafood sauce

1 tbsp olive oil

1 onion, sliced

1 red capsicum

1 clove garlic, crushed

1 red chili, seeded and finely chopped

½ tsp ground cumin

½ tsp ground coriander

14oz/400g canned tomatoes, undrained and mashed

Seafood Fettuccine

¼ cup dry white wine

1 tbsp tomato paste

5oz/145g calamari, cut into rings

5oz/145g cleaned fresh mussels in shells

1lb/500g uncooked large shrimp, peeled and deveined

4 tbsp fresh coriander, finely chopped

freshly ground black pepper

Method

Cook the fettuccine in a large pot of rapidly boiling water until al dente (cooked, but still with a bite to it) then drain well.

Put the olive oil, saffron, garlic, zest, juice, sugar and stock in a jar and whisk. Gently heat the mixture in a large, deep non stick frying pan until warm.

Cut the asparagus into 1½ in/4cm pieces and simmer in the olive oil mixture until bright green and just tender. Add the spring onions, tomatoes and fettuccine and toss gently to heat through. Remove from the heat and gently toss through the smoked salmon or trout, spinach, pine nuts and dill. Season with cracked black pepper and serve immediately.

Smoked Salmon, Asparagus and Lemon Fettuccine

Ingredients

1lb/500g fettuccine

2 tbsp extra virgin olive oil

pinch saffron

2 cloves garlic, crushed

1 tsp lemon zest

2oz/80ml lemon juice

1 tbsp sugar

1cup/250ml reduced salt chicken stock

10oz/300g asparagus

4 spring onions, sliced

4oz/100g semi-dried tomatoes

10oz/300g smoked salmon or smoked ocean trout, torn into large pieces

7oz/200g baby spinach leaves, washed

2oz/50g pine nuts, toasted

¼ cup chopped fresh dill

cracked black pepper to taste

Method

Bring a large pot of lightly salted water to a boil, add the pasta shells, and cook for 8-10 minutes, or until al dente; drain.

Heat the olive oil in a large pot over a medium heat. Sauté the mushrooms, spring onions, and garlic until tender. Stir in the shrimp, scallops, and crabmeat. Cook for 5 minutes, or until the shrimps are pink. Stir in the wine, lemon juice, and butter; cook for 5 minutes.

Toss the pasta with the seafood and parsley.

Ingredients

1lb/500g package medium shell pasta

6 tbsp olive oil

1 cup fresh mushrooms, sliced

¾ cup spring onions, minced

2 tbsp garlic, minced

1lb/500g medium shrimp, peeled and deveined

Seafood Piccata

1lb/500g scallops

1lb/500g crabmeat

2 cup dry white wine

6 tbsp fresh lemon juice

½ cup butter

¼ cup fresh chopped parsley

Method

Break the tuna into small bite-size pieces; put aside. Cook the pasta; drain and rinse with cold water. Combine all the dressing ingredients; mix well. Toss together the pasta, capsicum (peppers), beans, onions, tuna and dressing. If possible, refrigerate the salad overnight to allow flavours to blend. Serve cold.

Light Pasta Salad with Fresh Tuna Steak

Ingredients

16oz/455g Rotini, twists or spirals, uncooked

12oz/340g fresh tuna steak, cooked

3 tbsp olive or vegetable oil

4 tbsp Dijon-style mustard

6 tbsp rice wine vinegar

grated zest of 3 limes, finely chopped

6 fresh parsley sprigs, chopped

2 tbsp low-sodium soy sauce

3 garlic cloves, minced

1 tsp dried dill

1 cup chopped red capsicum (pepper)

1 cup green beans, julienne, blanched

⅔ cup Spanish onion, pared, thinly sliced

Method

Place the tomatoes in a bowl and pour over boiling water. Leave for 30 seconds, then peel, deseed and chop.

Heat 3 tbsp of oil in a large heavy-based saucepan, then gently fry the garlic and chili for 1 minute to release their flavours. Add the fish, oregano and seasoning, then pour over the wine. Bring to boil, then reduce the heat and simmer, covered, for 5 minutes, turning the fish once. Add the tomatoes and cook for additional

5 minutes, uncovered, until the fish is cooked through and the tomatoes have softened. Season to taste.

Meanwhile, cook the pasta in plenty of boiling salted water, until tender but still firm to the bite, then drain. Transfer to a warmed serving bowl, toss with the remaining oil and then spoon over the sauce.

Garnish with parsley.

Penne and Monkfish in Tomato Sauce

Ingredients

9oz/250g ripe tomatoes

6 tbsp extra virgin olive oil

1 clove garlic, chopped

1 tsp crushed dried chilies

12oz/350g monkfish fillets,

skin removed, cut into

1in/2.5cm chunks

1 tbsp dried oregano

7fl oz/200ml dry white wine

12oz/350g dried pasta quills (penne)

chopped fresh parsley to garnish

salt and black pepper

Method

Cook the fettuccine in boiling water in a large saucepan following the packet directions. Drain, set aside and keep warm.

To make the sauce, blanch peas in boiling water for 2 minutes. Refresh under cold running water, drain and set aside. Place the wine in a large frying pan and bring to boil. Stir in 1 cup cream and boil until sauce reduces and thickens. Place 4 slices of the smoked salmon, spring onions and remaining cream in a food processor and purée. Stir the smoked salmon mixture into sauce and cook until sauce is hot.

Cut the remaining salmon slices into strips. Add the salmon strips and peas to the sauce and season to taste with black pepper. Spoon the sauce over the fettuccine and toss to combine. Serve immediately.

Ingredients

1lb/500g fettuccine

Smoked Salmon Sauce

4oz/115g fresh or frozen peas

¼ cup white wine

1¼ cup heavy cream

8 slices smoked salmon

3 spring onions, finely chopped

freshly ground black pepper

Smoked Salmon Fettuccine

Method

Cook the pasta in boiling salted water until just cooked (al dente).

Drain, and rinse in cold water.

Heat 2 tbsp of the oil in a pan, add the garlic and chili,

and cook for 2-3 minutes. Return the cooked pasta to the pan,

add the remaining ingredients, and heat through.

Serve immediately with Parmesan cheese.

Penne with Tuna, Olives and Artichokes

Ingredients

1lb/500g penne pasta

6 tbsp olive oil

2 cloves garlic, minced

3 chilies, seeded and finely chopped

1 cup black olives, seeded

13oz/410g can artichokes

2 tbsp capers, chopped finely

14oz/440g can tuna, drained

Method

Cook the fettuccine in boiling water in a large saucepan following the packet directions. Drain, set aside and keep warm.

To make the sauce, melt the butter in a large frying pan and cook red capsicum (pepper) and spring onions for 1-2 minutes. Add the cream and bring to the boil, then reduce the heat and simmer for 5 minutes or until sauce reduces slightly and thickens.

Stir the scallops into the sauce and cook for 2-3 minutes or until the scallops are opaque. Season to taste with the black pepper. Place the fettuccine in a warm serving bowl, top with sauce and sprinkle with parsley.

Quick Fettuccine with Scallops

Ingredients

1lb/500g fettuccine

1 tbsp fresh parsley, finely chopped

scallop sauce

1oz/30g butter

1 red capsicum (pepper), cut into strips

2 spring onions, finely chopped

1 cup heavy cream

1lb/500g scallops

freshly ground black pepper

Method

Cook the spaghettini in boiling water with a little oil (until al dente). Run under cold water, until cold, and set aside.

Heat half the oil and cook the garlic on a low heat, until beginning to change colour. Add the chili and tomato, and cook for a few minutes.

Add the clams, parsley, lemon juice, remaining oil, spaghettini and a little of the water used to cook the clams, and heat through, for additional 5 minutes. Season with salt and black ground pepper.

Ingredients

13oz/410g spaghettini

2½fl oz/85ml olive oil

4 cloves garlic, sliced

4 red chilies, finely chopped

2 cups tomato, finely diced

21oz/650g canned baby clams, or fresh if available

1/3 cup parsley, chopped

juice of 2 lemons

salt & freshly ground black pepper

Spaghettini with Baby Clams, Chili and Garlic

Note

If using fresh clams, wash under running water (scraping the shells with a sharp knife or scourer). Put them in a large pan with a little water over a gentle heat, until they open. Discard any that do not open.

67

71

Method

Cook the ravioli in boiling water in a large saucepan following packet directions. Drain, set aside and keep warm.

To make the sauce, heat the oil in a frying pan and cook the onion and garlic over a medium heat for 4-5 minutes or until the onion is soft. Stir in the tomatoes, tomato paste, wine and sugar. Bring to the boil, then add the tuna, parsley and dill. Reduce the heat and simmer for 10 minutes or until the sauce reduces and thickens.

Place the ravioli on a warmed serving platter, spoon the sauce over, sprinkle with Parmesan cheese and serve immediately.

Ravioli with Tuna Sauce

Ingredients

13oz/370g fresh or frozen spinach ravioli

2 tbsp grated Parmesan cheese

Tuna Tomato Sauce

1 tsp olive oil

1 onion, finely chopped

1 clove garlic, crushed

14oz/400g canned tomatoes, undrained and mashed

1 tbsp tomato paste

1 tbsp dry red wine

1 tsp sugar

14oz/400g canned tuna, drained and flaked

1 tbsp finely chopped fresh parsley

1 tbsp finely chopped fresh dill

freshly ground black pepper

73

Method

Preheat the oven to 350°F/180°C. Heat the oil in a large frying pan, add the leek and cook until tender. Stir in the tomatoes and tomato paste. Cook until mixture boils. Simmer uncovered until the sauce is slightly thickened. Stir in the shrimp and fish pieces, cover and cook over low heat for about 5 minutes.

Cook the lasagne in a saucepan of boiling water al dente. Place lasagne in a large bowl of cool water until ready to use.

Spoon 1/3 of the sauce into the bottom of a 2in/5cm deep casserole dish. Drain lasagne sheets and arrange a single layer over the seafood sauce. Spoon another 1/3 of the sauce over the lasagne, and top with another layer of lasagne.

Spread the remaining 1/3 of sauce over lasagne and top with mozzarella cheese. Bake in an oven for 40 minutes.

Seafood Lasagne

Ingredients

2 tbsp olive oil

1 leek, white part only, finely chopped

14oz/400g chopped canned tomatoes

2 tbsp tomato paste

1 lb/500g uncooked shrimps, shelled
and deveined, cut into small pieces

9oz/255g boneless white fish fillets,
cut into small pieces

15 sheets spinach lasagne

4oz/115g mozzarella cheese, thinly sliced

Method

Peel and devein the shrimps, leaving the tails intact. Pat the scallops

dry with paper towel.

Cook the spaghetti in a large pot of rapidly boiling water until al dente

(cooked but still with a bite to it). Drain, cover and keep warm.

Heat the olive oil spread and olive oil in a large, deep fry pan and cook

the shrimps and scallops in batches over a high heat just until tender.

Remove and keep warm.

Add the garlic, onion and chili to the pan and cook over a medium heat until

the onion is soft. Stir in the wine and bring to a boil, stirring to release any

juices that may be stuck to the bottom of the pan. Boil until reduced by half.

Add the tomatoes, zest, sugar and chives to the pan and cook just until

the tomato is warmed through.

Add the shrimp, scallops and spaghetti and toss to combine.

Serve with crusty bread.

Spicy Shrimp and Scallop Spaghetti

Ingredients

1lb/500g green shrimps	1 small red chili, finely chopped
½ lb/250g scallops without roe	4fl oz/125ml dry white wine
12 oz/350g tubular spaghetti	2 large vine ripened tomatoes,
1oz/30g olive oil spread	seeded and finely chopped
2 tsp olive oil	1 tsp lemon zest
2 cloves garlic, crushed	1 tsp orange zest
3 spring onions, sliced	1 tsp white sugar
	1 tbsp chopped fresh chives

Method

Prepare the pasta according to the package directions. While the pasta is cooking, stir together in a large bowl, all the other ingredients, including reserved pineapple juice. When the pasta is done, drain and rinse in cold water; drain again.

Toss the pasta in with the other ingredients, season with salt and pepper and serve immediately.

Shells with Shrimp and Fruit

Ingredients

18oz/510g medium shells, Mostaccioli or other medium pasta shape, uncooked

12oz/340g cooked, peeled medium shrimp

1x 16oz can chickpeas (garbanzo beans), drained

1 x 20oz/570g can pineapple chunks in juice, drained, 2 tbsp juice reserved

2 large, ripe mangoes or peaches, peeled and diced

1 bunch spring onions, sliced

2 tbsp chopped fresh coriander

2 tbsp fresh lime juice

salt and pepper to taste

Method

Cook the pasta according to the package directions. While the pasta is cooking, heat the oil in a non-stick pan and sauté the garlic carefully to avoid burning.

Add the oysters and pour the white wine over. Bring to boil. Add the clam juice and the evaporated milk, bring back to boiling and cook for 3 more minutes. Add the spinach to the pan and cook until wilted.

When the pasta is done, drain and combine with oyster and spinach mixture.

Add the basil, parsley and salt and pepper to taste. Serve immediately.

Shells with Oysters and Spinach

Ingredients

8oz/225g medium shells, elbow macaroni or other medium pasta shape, uncooked

1 tbsp olive or vegetable oil

3 cloves garlic, chopped

4oz/115g select oysters or 12 oysters, fresh shucked, liquid reserved, or one 4oz bottle oysters with juice

2fl oz/55ml white wine

4fl oz/115ml clam juice

2fl oz/55ml evaporated skim milk

8oz/225g fresh spinach, washed, hard stems removed

6 fresh basil leaves, chopped

½ cup parsley, chopped

salt and white pepper to taste

Method

Mix the salmon, 1 tablespoon of eggwhite, the cream and the dill well in a food processor, until it becomes a mousse.

Dust a cutting board or the kitchen counter with corn flour and place the wonton sheets on it in rows of four.

Spread eggwhite all around the edges of every other sheet and put a teaspoon of the salmon mousse in the center of the other sheets. Place the sheet with eggwhite on top of that with salmon mousse and press the edges together so that they look like small cushions.

Fill a pan half-full with water, add 1 teaspoon of oil and bring the water to boil. Cook all the ravioli, in batches, for 2-3 minutes. Set them apart and cover them with cling film.

Melt the butter for the sauce in a pan, add the butter and boil this for 1 minute.

Add the wine and stir until it becomes a smooth mass. Then mix in the cream and the lemon juice. Bring the whole to a boil and let the sauce boil down until it is thick.

Finally, add the dill and some salt and pepper to the sauce and pour the sauce over the ravioli.

Salmon Ravioli with Lemon-Dill Sauce

Ingredients	For the lemon-dill sauce
5 oz/125 g smoked salmon shreds	1 tbsp butter, 1 tbsp flour
1 eggwhite	6fl oz/185 ml white wine
1½ tbsp heavy cream	6fl oz/185 ml heavy cream
2 tsp fresh dill, coarsely chopped	juice of ½ a lemon
2-3 tbsp corn flour	2 tbsp dill, coarsely chopped
32 wonton sheets	salt, freshly ground
1 tsp oil	pepper, freshly ground

Method

Melt butter in a saucepan over a medium heat, stir in flour and cook for 1 minute. Remove pan from heat, add mustard and slowly stir in milk and lemon juice. Return pan to heat and cook, stirring constantly, for 5 minutes or until sauce boils and thickens.

Stir in tuna, pasta, half the cheese and black pepper to taste. Spoon mixture into a greased shallow ovenproof dish, sprinkle with remaining cheese and bake for 20 minutes or until cheese melts and top is golden.

Ingredients

2oz/60g butter

2 tbsp flour

1 tsp dry mustard

1½ cups/12fl oz/375ml milk

2 tsp lemon juice

7oz/220g canned tuna, drained and flaked

3oz/90g elbow macaroni or other small pasta, cooked

4oz/125g grated tasty cheese (mature Cheddar)

freshly ground black pepper

Tuna and Macaroni Bake

Note

A great way to use up leftover pasta, this

traditional family favourite is also delicious

made with canned salmon, ham leftover

cooked chicken or turkey in place of the tuna.

Method

To make the sauce, cover the plum tomatoes with boiling water and leave for 30 seconds. Drain, peel and deseed them and chop the flesh.

Heat the oil in a saucepan. Add the onion, garlic, celery, pepper and mushrooms and cook for 5 minutes or until softened, stirring occasionally. Mix in the chopped tomatoes, sun-dried tomatoes, red wine, tomato purée and black pepper. Bring to a boil, cover, then reduce the heat and simmer for 20 minutes or until the vegetables are tender, stirring occasionally.

Cook the tagliatelle, meanwhile, according to the packet instructions and until just firm to the bite. Stir the mussels into the tomato sauce, increase the heat slightly and cook, uncovered, for 5 minutes or until piping hot, stirring occasionally. Drain the pasta, add to the sauce with the basil and toss well. Garnish with the basil leaves and serve immediately.

Tagliatelle with Tomato and Mussels

Ingredients

12oz/350g dried tagliatelle

8oz/225g cooked shelled mussels

2 tbsp chopped fresh basil,

plus whole leaves to garnish

For the sauce

1lb 9oz/700g ripe plum tomatoes

1 tbsp olive oil

1 onion, finely chopped

2 cloves garlic, finely chopped

2 sticks celery, finely chopped

1 red pepper, deseeded and finely chopped

4oz/125g button mushrooms, finely chopped

4 sun-dried tomatoes, soaked,

drained and finely chopped

6 tbsp red wine

2 tbsp tomato purée

black pepper

Method

Cook the pasta in boiling water in a large saucepan following the packet directions. Drain, rinse under cold running water, then drain again and set aside to cool completely.

Cut the anchovies in half lengthwise. Wrap an anchovy strip around each olive. Place the pasta, anchovy-wrapped olives, tuna, parsley and chives in a salad bowl.

To make the dressing, place mustard, garlic, vinegar, oil and black pepper to taste in a screwtop jar and shake well. Pour the dressing over salad and toss to combine. Top with egg wedges.

Ingredients

9oz/255g wholemeal pasta spirals

6 canned anchovies, drained

12 black olives

7oz/200g canned tuna, drained

1 tbsp chopped fresh parsley

1 tbsp snipped fresh chives

1 hard-boiled egg, cut in wedges

Tuna Anchovy Salad

Mustard Dressing

1 tsp Dijon mustard

1 clove garlic, crushed

1 tbsp white wine vinegar

¼ cup olive oil

freshly ground black pepper

Method

Scrub the mussels under cold running water, pull away any beards and discard any mussels that are open or damaged. Place 2 tbsp of the oil in a large heavy-based saucepan, then add the mussels. Cook, covered, for 2-4 minutes, until the mussels open, shaking the pan frequently.

Discard any mussels that do not open. Reserve 12 mussels in their shells for garnishing. Detach the remaining mussels from their shells and set aside, discarding the shells.

Cook the pasta in plenty of boiling salted water, until tender but still firm to the bite, then drain. Meanwhile, place the remaining oil, the wine, parsley, garlic and chili in a large heavy-based frying pan and bring to boil. Cook for 2 minutes to boil off the alcohol. Stir the mussels and pasta into the oil and chili mixture and toss for 30 seconds to heat through. Serve garnished with the reserved mussels.

Spaghetti with Mussels

Ingredients

4lb 8oz/2kg mussels

6 tbsp extra virgin olive oil

12oz/350g dried spaghetti

4fl oz/100ml dry white wine

2oz/50g chopped fresh flat-leaf parsley

2 cloves garlic, chopped

1 tsp crushed dried chilies

salt

Method

Sauté the onion in olive oil until soft. Add the garlic and wine and boil vigorously for 2 minutes. Reduce heat, add the tomatoes, parsley, oregano, salt and pepper to taste.

Add the calamari, cover and cook for 45 minutes, stirring from time to time. Add the mushrooms and continue cooking 5 minutes.

Cook the spaghetti, drain. Toss with the sauce and serve.

Spaghetti with Calamari Sauce

Ingredients

1 onion, chopped	½ tsp dried oregano
2 tbsp olive oil	freshly ground black pepper
½ tsp finely chopped garlic	2¼lb/1kg calamari, cleaned and sliced into rings
1½ cups white wine	8oz/115g mushrooms, sliced
4oz/115g chopped canned tomatoes	1lb/500g spaghetti
2 tbsp chopped fresh parsley	salt

Method

Boil the pasta in boiling water in a large saucepan according to the instructions on the packet. Drain well and put the pasta into a large serving dish.

Add the tuna, watercress, olives, lime zest, ginger, oil and lime juice to the warm pasta and mix.

Serve immediately.

Spaghetti with Tuna-Watercress

Ingredients

1lb/500g spaghetti

1lb/500g tuna steaks, thinly sliced

1 bunch of water cress, leaves

(stalks are not used)

4 oz/115g black olives

1 tbsp lime rind, finely grated

2 tsp fresh ginger, finely grated

2fl oz/60ml balsamic or red wine vinegar

1 tbsp olive oil

2 tbsp lime juice

Index